Original title:
Garden of Ghosts

Copyright © 2025 Creative Arts Management OÜ
All rights reserved.

Author: Juliette Kensington
ISBN HARDBACK: 978-1-80567-051-3
ISBN PAPERBACK: 978-1-80567-131-2

The Fragrant Graveyard

In the shadows, petals sigh,
Worms dance by in the dirt nearby.
Marigolds chuckle, rosebush grins,
As the earth spins with playful sins.

Toadstools wiggle under moonlight,
Mice don hats in the soft night.
Daisies gossip, a wild affair,
With honeybees buzzing without a care.

Whispers Carried by the Breeze

Breezes giggle through the trees,
Tickling leaves, a joyful tease.
Squirrels in top hats, oh so dapper,
Juggling acorns with a flapper.

The wind carries tales of jest,
Of plants who thought they were the best.
With each rustle, secrets spill,
In this quirky realm, time stands still.

The Remains of Summer

Lemonade stands in ghostly glow,
Picnics linger, but it's time to go.
Sandwiches squabble, chips on parade,
In this laughter, memories won't fade.

Faded sun hats, a jaunty sight,
Chasing shadows, embracing night.
With jokes shared 'neath the twinkling stars,
The echoes of laughter linger like scars.

Lush Landscapes of Longing

In the twilight, a longing play,
Laughter spills in a backward sway.
Ghostly flowers reach for fun,
Buds that blossom with each pun.

Caterpillars in a conga line,
Mimicking dancers with a twist of vine.
Frogs in tuxedos croak a tune,
While fireflies sway, a glowing boon.

Secrets Beneath the Soil

Worms in bow ties, dancing round,
Roots do the tango, underground.
Weeds in whispers, sharing old jokes,
The plants giggle, even the oaks.

Sunflowers gossip, peeking at bugs,
Laughing softly, giving them hugs.
The carrots chuckle, their tops all green,
Roots full of secrets, seldom seen.

Ethereal Blooms of Yesteryear

Petals that wink, sharing old tales,
Daisies declare they're on pirate gales.
Tulips in costumes, wearing old hats,
The violets chuckle at catty spats.

Dandelions blowing, full of cheer,
Whispering laughter, no hint of fear.
The phantoms of florals, dicier than cake,
Cheering up night when the shadows quake.

Forgotten Pathways of Light

Paths made of sparkles lead the way,
Where shadows strut and giggle in play.
A moonbeam slips, trips on a vine,
Chortles and chuckles, the stars align.

The lantern bugs tell tales of the past,
Of silliness blunders and shadows cast.
Echoes of laughter dance through the air,
Even the ghosts have flair to spare.

The Wailing Vines

Vines in a tangle, throwing a fit,
Crying for help, but they're kind of lit.
A swing and a sway, a comedic scene,
Pretending they're old at just fifteen.

Ghosts holding vines, trying to tie,
Flapping and flailing, oh what a high!
They trip on their sheets, in a chuckle-storm,
Among the old roses, a sight so warm.

In the Shade of Lost Moments

In the corners of laughter, they play,
Faded tunes from another day.
Tickling the petals, they glide,
Whispers of humor, we cannot hide.

Jokes in the wind, swirling so fast,
Echoes of giggles from the past.
They dance in the shadows, light as a feather,
Mixing up memories like a grand jester.

Silly faces bloom in the night,
Turning memories into sheer delight.
They pull at our heartstrings, still and thin,
Knowing too well where we've been.

With a wink and a nod, they tease,
A jest in the air, a playful breeze.
For in every chuckle, there's something to find,
Laughter lives on, though time is unkind.

The Darkened Floral Trail

Petals giggle in the autumn gloom,
Floral mischief is sure to bloom.
The moonlight jokes with the trees,
Whispers of pranks ride the breeze.

Approaching the path where shadows meet,
The flowers conspire, no small feat.
Their roots twist and turn with glee,
Playing hide and seek, just wait and see.

Bright colors laugh where none can tread,
Silly thoughts dance in every head.
The moment you stop to take a glance,
Petunias chuckle as they prance.

Once in a while, they'll poke and prod,
Making you question the evening nod.
For even the wild can't help but smile,
With nature's jokes, stay a while.

Resurgence of the Ghostly Hue

In shades of gray, they pop and bop,
Cheeky whispers that never stop.
Bright hues peering from behind the veil,
Each hue with a story, a twist or a tail.

Who knew that ghosts could wear such flair?
With polka dots, they float in the air.
Colorful antics, they just can't cease,
A tapestry woven of laughter and peace.

Tickled pink in the early light,
They spin around, making day from night.
As shadows chuckle and sunlight beams,
They mock the worries, the tangled dreams.

With every giggle, a burst of cheer,
Awakening memories, drawing near.
Amidst the laughter, the colors sway,
Bringing joy to the end of day.

The Solstice of Memory's Shade

As daylight dances on the grass,
Ghostly whispers make moments pass.
They play tag in the fading sun,
Laughing and leaping, oh what fun!

Each shadow flickers, a smile wide,
Remnants of laughter, they can't hide.
A prankster's wink, a sudden thrill,
Hopscotch on memories, what a skill!

Time ticks lightly, a teasing tune,
Dares of laughter beneath the moon.
Even in silence, they burst with cheer,
For every memory, they're always near.

In the twilight where shadows dream,
Silly shades flicker like a stream.
With playful intent, they spin and twirl,
In the softest light, watch them whirl.

Ripples on the Surface of Silence

In the hush of the night, a whispering breeze,
A ghostly giggle floats through the trees.
The shadows are laughing, they dance and they twirl,
Through the quiet they skip, like a joyful squirrel.

In the moonlight they prance, wearing hats made of mist,
Bumping into each other, they turn and they twist.
A spirit with humor, a cheeky little sprite,
Shakes hands with the darkness, they party til light.

With jokes from the past and tales of delight,
The echoes of laughter blend with the night.
Their playful antics are hard to ignore,
As they dance in the twilight, they're always asking for more.

The silence might tremble, but they have no fear,
For every soft chuckle's a sign they're all here.
Ripples of joy paint the air all around,
In the stillness they twinkle; oh, what fun can be found!

The Unfurling of Shadowy Blooms

In the garden of night, where the shadows are bright,
Faded petals of laughter bloom, what a sight!
They chuckle and shimmer when no one's awake,
But trip on the roots of the jokes that they make.

With a tickle of fog, they rustle and sway,
Whispering puns in a ghostly ballet.
A specter with flair and a penchant for fun,
Crafts a crown of green ivy, who says it's just one?

Each bloom tells a tale of the jester's old days,
With winks and with giggles, in humorous ways.
A laugh in the vines grows heavier still,
As each shadowy bloom seems to giggle at will.

The petals all soar, as they dance in a line,
Twirling together in the moonlit shine.
A festival of phantoms, they laugh through the gloom,
In a riot of fun, where the shadowy blooms loom.

A Symphony of Faint Echoes

In the twilight's embrace, a chorus takes flight,
With giggles and chuckles that blend in the night.
The echoes are ticklish, they prance through the air,
Like whispers of mischief in a world laid bare.

Notes from the phantoms play tricks on the breeze,
As fiddle and laughter sail through the trees.
With a stir of old tales and a wink of surprise,
The shadows sing songs that spark the skies.

A symphony played on a stage made of mist,
With instruments fashioned from dreams that persist.
Bells of the moonlight ring softly and sweet,
As feathery giggles dance down to your feet.

Each note carries whimsy, each chord comes alive,
A merriment flourishes, ready to thrive.
In this waltz of the whispers, the fun never ends,
Where echoes of laughter are ghosts, and are friends.

Shadows in the Twilight Dance

As the sun bids goodnight, the shadows take sway,
In the twilight they gather, ready to play.
They tango with whispers, they cha-cha with cheer,
With cookies of starlight and smiles without fear.

A phantom parade steps out one by one,
Wearing fabrics of midnight, under the sun.
They twirl on their toes, hats askew on their heads,
Joining in laughter where silence once spreads.

With each funny misstep, a chuckle resounds,
As they frolic through forests, their fun knows no bounds.
Beneath the soft glow of a flickering flame,
Each shade joins the jive, never feeling the same.

In the dusk's gentle hug, their secrets unfold,
A comedy of spirits, fearless and bold.
Shadows may linger, but with joy in their stance,
They lead every moment to a giddy dance!

Lurking Beneath the Rosebush

In shadows where the roses sway,
A ghostly cat decides to play.
It chases dreams with furry grace,
Leaving flowers in a messy place.

The spirits dance on petals bright,
While gnomes hold conferences at night.
With laughter that you cannot hear,
They toast to all who bring them cheer.

A snail in armor takes the stage,
Reciting poetry from a dusty page.
The daisies giggle, twist and shout,
As the snail serenades the cloudy bout.

Underneath the rose's throne,
A buried treasure, all alone.
But when you dig to claim your prize,
A ghostly laugh is your surprise.

The Otherworldly Grove

In a grove where daisies grin,
The playful sprites begin to spin.
With wild hair and twinkling eyes,
They pull the roots and wear them like ties.

A ghostly squirrel, ever so sly,
Offers hugs to passersby.
With nutty jokes that seem absurd,
You can't help but laugh, it's plain as a bird.

They host a ball beneath the moon,
Where shadows waltz to a haunting tune.
With owls in hats and mice in skirts,
Their midnight feast is full of quirks.

But tread lightly on the buzzing path,
For the ghost bees love a good laugh.
They'll tickle your feet and make you squeal,
While plotting how to steal your meal!

Twilight Serenade of the Unseen

As twilight sings an eerie song,
The unseen troupe starts to throng.
Invisible hands pluck the tunes,
A symphony of giggles and swoons.

The fireflies join the grand parade,
While shadows prance in masquerade.
With each flicker, they twist and twirl,
Summoning laughter from the world.

A ghost on stilts trips over a vine,
His laugh echoes, "I'm just fine!"
In a pirouette, he dances away,
Only to bump into a pile of hay.

As stars peek from the blanket of dusk,
The party blooms with fragrant musk.
Spirits toast with ancient chews,
All in jest, with no real blues.

Mysteries Amongst the Ivy

Amidst the ivy, secrets creep,
Whispers of a cat that never sleeps.
With sly grins and swishing tails,
They chase the wind and weave their tales.

A lizard dressed in polka dots,
Welcomes all to curious plots.
With riddles wrapped in vines so tight,
They'll have you laughing until light.

An owl in glasses reads the runes,
While everyone dances to old tunes.
With a wiggle here and a wriggle there,
The ivy giggles, full of flair.

So, tiptoe through this playful maze,
Where every turn is full of praise.
For the mysteries that you shall find,
Are wrapped in laughs for the merry mind.

Whispers of the Forgotten

In a patch where weeds do dance,
Old socks and spoons take their chance.
Each step stirs polite debate,
On which ghostie is first to mate.

A scarecrow waves with a funny hat,
While a gopher plans a ghostly spat.
They argue over who's the best,
At haunting humans, much to jest.

Shades Beneath the Petals

Bees buzz in polka-dot brigade,
Sipping nectar in grand parade.
Floral spirits tease and twirl,
While bugs break out in a tango swirl.

A butterfly with a monocle grand,
Mocks a slug dressed in green band.
They waltz beneath the mushroom dome,
In this quirky place they call home.

Echoes in the Overgrown

Old boots rest 'neath leafy shrouds,
While whispers float like fluffy clouds.
A marigold speaks with a wink,
To a daisy caught in a thought-filled shrink.

Lawn chairs hold their ghostly crowd,
With laughter lost beneath a shroud.
They share jokes about their fate,
As the sun sets, it's getting late.

Shadows of Memory

A squirrel, wearing a tiny crown,
Directs the shadows up and down.
They play hide-and-seek with glee,
In this odd patch of memory.

Fences chirp with old complaints,
While wandering weeds pull off their pranks.
The old gnarled roots just can't recall,
If they ever meant to grow at all.

Ethereal Blooms of the Unforgotten.

In the corner, blooms giggle and sway,
Beards of moss join in their play.
A gnome with a grin, tossing seeds of cheer,
Where magic's a jest and laughter's near.

Chortles emerge from the daisies' wake,
As butterflies dance, they all partake.
A waltz of whispers that tickles the breeze,
In this patch of glee, even shadows tease.

Whispers in the Moonlit Thicket

In the thicket where shadows poke fun,
Laughter echoes under the moonlit run.
A hare in a top hat, sipping his tea,
Winks at the owls, as merry as can be.

The stars join in with a twinkling jest,
While crickets chirp tales of unwelcome guests.
A mischief of spirits, quick on their toes,
Play hide and seek with the weeds as they doze.

Shadows of Forgotten Blossoms

Once faded petals wear a funny face,
With puns so silly, they lighten the place.
An old scarlet rose flirts with the breeze,
While daisies gossip in silly decrees.

The bumblebees hum with a comic tone,
As footprints of spirits make mischief their own.
A whispering vine tells tales of delight,
In this comedy of life, every moment feels bright.

Echoes Beneath the Willow

Beneath the willow, a jester resides,
Tickling the branches, where silliness hides.
With shadows that shimmy and giggle with glee,
Even the moon bends down for a peek.

The breeze tells jokes only the flowers can hear,
As the willowy dancer spins without fear.
A punchline of petals floats gently in air,
In this whimsical realm, nothing's too rare.

Dancing with the Ethereal Mists

In the haze they swirl and sway,
With silly hats they dance and play.
A ghostly jig beneath the moon,
They've got the moves, oh what a tune!

With poltergeist flair, they spin around,
Mischievous giggles, a haunting sound.
They tease the flowers, give them a scare,
Spilling secrets on the midnight air.

Invisible friends with quirky charm,
Whispering jokes that keep us warm.
A spectral bash, come join the fun,
Floating 'til dawn, when the night is done!

So if you glimpse a shimmer tonight,
Join the dance, don't take flight.
For in the mists, laughter gleams,
In a waltz of shadows, we weave our dreams.

The Hollowed Seedbed

In a plot where mischief grows,
Seeds of laughter, who really knows?
The plants wore coats, they pranced about,
Exchanging jokes with a cheeky shout.

The carrots giggle as they sprout,
While radishes roll with wary doubt.
"I'm just so leafy, aren't you seed?"
Yet all agree, they're quite the breed!

The onions cry, "We're way too bold!"
While mushrooms dance, all dressed in gold.
A patch so wild, it breaks all rules,
These are the silliest of garden ghouls.

So if you wander where they thrive,
You'll find no gloom, only jive.
For in this bed of fun and cheer,
The hollows whisper, "Stay right here!"

Echos of the Hollow Hedge

From a distance, the hedge does call,
With mysterious whispers, a ghostly sprawl.
What secrets hide in thickets tight?
It's just the laughter of the night!

Crickets sing and specters leap,
In shadows deep, they seldom sleep.
The branches sway with a knowing grin,
As echoes dance, they twirl and spin.

A sprightly breeze will tease your hair,
Making you wonder, 'Is someone there?'
But peek closely, and you may find,
The ghouls are jesters, playful and kind.

So join the laughter near that hedge,
Let go your thoughts, take a pledge.
For in their tricks, the fun ensues,
With echoes swirling in playful hues.

The Lamenting Lily

A lily pouted in the moon's soft glow,
"Why do these ghouls steal my show?"
With petals drooping, 'neath sighs she wilted,
While shadows snickered, her dreams were quilted.

"Oh dear lily, don't be dismayed,
We're here for laughs, and games to be played!"
The phantom buds rushed in with zest,
"Let's have some fun, you need a rest!"

They pranked the breeze, made ticklish air,
And turned her frown into a stare.
She giggled softly, swayed with grace,
As dancing specters embraced the space.

Now the lily, bright with gleeful cheer,
Swaying gently, with friends near.
No more lamenting, just joyous blooms,
For in the night, laughter consumes.

Remnants of a Fragrant Past

In the yard where laughter faded,
Silly scents of socks paraded.
A daffodil wearing a beret,
Told me jokes that made me sway.

The basil whispers stories old,
Of mischief and a brave chef bold.
Tomatoes played their hide and seek,
With thyme that giggled, feeling sleek.

A trumpet vine danced with great flair,
As gnomes played tag without a care.
The moon peeked in, grinning wide,
At the chaos where the blooms abide.

But in this patch of memories bright,
Even weeds know how to take flight.
With tangled roots and cheeky blooms,
They sing their songs among the fumes.

Twilight Conversations with Shadows

In twilight where the shadows creep,
I heard the plants begin to peep.
A fern cracked jokes, so very sly,
While daisies winked and wondered why.

The hedges busily conspired,
While the oak tree seemed so tired.
With branches stretched, he let out a sigh,
"Why do the crickets always pry?"

A blooming rose, with thorns so sharp,
Started singing to an off-key harp.
The nightshade joined in, soft and low,
With tales of how the weeds can grow.

And as the stars began to blink,
The shadows paused to stop and think.
With laughter echoing through the dark,
They tossed around a ghostly spark.

The Memory Orchard

In an orchard filled with glee,
Apples giggled on a tree.
Pears told tales of silly slips,
While peaches planned their dancing trips.

Bananas with their peels so bright,
Slipped and stumbled, what a sight!
Citrus fruits made funny puns,
As cherries tried to catch the sun.

The shadows danced beneath the boughs,
As owls joined in, sharing vows.
"Let's make a fruit salad of mirth,
And serenade the quiet earth!"

With every laugh that filled the air,
The ghosts of fruits spun without care.
Their joyous roots brought to life,
The sweetest moments, void of strife.

Ethereal Roots of Nostalgia

In the yard where memories bloom,
A squash once claimed it owned the room.
The carrots laughed with leafy friends,
In tales of ghosts on playful bends.

The radish giggled, pink and round,
Said secrets hide beneath the ground.
The onions chimed in with their tears,
While whispers flew through time and fears.

At twilight's touch, the shadows twirled,
With shadows of laughter, joy unfurled.
They shared their tricks and silly pranks,
In the realm of roots and fragrant ranks.

As dusk descended, spirits swayed,
In the awkward waltz that memories played.
Each echo painted scenes of cheer,
A funny world that felt so near.

Echoing Serenity in the Glade

In the quiet nooks, laughter sings,
Where shadows dance on invisible wings.
Flowers giggle like they've met a jester,
While trees listen close, like a seasoned tester.

A whispering breeze shares a cheeky joke,
As mushrooms chuckle, in silence they choke.
Ferns sway to rhythm, a silly charade,
In this tranquil spot where pranks are displayed.

The Weeping Shrub

A shrub with tears but a smile so wide,
Cries for the snail who lost his pride.
He slipped on a leaf, so slick and so green,
Now he's the legend of the scene.

With weepy branches, he scoffs and he shrieks,
'Why fret, little friend, it's just for a week!'
The blooms all chuckle, they know he's no fool,
In a world of their own, they bend every rule.

Scent of the Unremembered

Fragrant breezes bring tales from the past,
Of socks lost in laundry, and shadows cast.
The daisies whisper of time gone awry,
Whilst bees battle memories that just seem to fly.

A sprig of thyme claims to hold all the spice,
Of laughter and mischief, oh, isn't it nice?
They hum to each other, a symphony sweet,
Where nothing's forgotten, and all's a fun feat.

Veiled in Silver Mist

A mist that giggles as it rolls on by,
Cloaks every flower, a playful sly tie.
The tulips are winking, their petals aflare,
While clouds above chuckle, with nary a care.

Ghostly whispers play games of peek-a-boo,
They trick the sun into joining the crew.
Here, hilarity reigns amid dusky fogs,
In a world of frolic, for owls and for dogs.

When the Nightshade Whispers

In the moonlight, shadows dance,
Cabbages plot their devilish prance.
Carrots giggle in their patches,
While squashes hide beneath the hatches.

Beans in pajamas whisper tales,
Of ghostly beans with phantom sails.
They spin their yarns of frightful fun,
As radishes race, trying to run!

The celery sways, all dressed in green,
As specters play tag through unseen.
A pumpkin grins, with a toothy sneer,
"Boo! It's just me!" he hollers cheer.

So if you wander after dark,
Beware the garden's silly spark.
For in this patch of leafy fun,
The spirits play till night is done!

Chasing Glimmers of Ghostly Light

Fireflies flicker, a ghostly chase,
Among the blooms, they dart and race.
A playful breeze makes the branches sway,
While shadows leap and giggles play.

Lilies hiding secrets bright,
Whisper softly through the night.
"Catch us, catch us!" they seem to tease,
As butterflies drift with effortless ease.

The moon grins wide, a cheeky guide,
As wand'ring souls in flowers hide.
They tickle the petals, fill them with cheer,
With laughter echoing, so near, so near!

So come along with jest and light,
Into the glimmers, bold and bright.
Where every bloom and shadow blooms,
Is a world of giggles that surely looms!

The Restless Briar

Thorns and brambles, all in a row,
Plotting mischief in the evening glow.
With gnarled fingers, they pull and tug,
Beware the prickle, it's a wily bug!

The roses laugh, with petals wide,
As thistle chuckles, full of pride.
"Ouch!" says the daisy, "Watch where you poke,
You thorny rascal, you're such a joke!"

Amidst the thickets, whispers collide,
Frogs serenade the night with pride.
A jester's hat atop a hedge,
Sings silly songs from a leafy ledge.

So take a stroll, but hold on tight,
To silly ways in the starry night.
For every briar that pricks and jabs,
Is just a riddle from the garden's gabs!

Phantoms Behind the Grasses

Beneath the blades, the phantoms creep,
In a game of hide and seek, they leap.
Fuzzy bunnies giggle and flee,
As ghostly whispers call with glee.

The daisies roll their tiny eyes,
At specters who plot surprise pies.
"Boo!" says a gourd, with a jolly grin,
"Join our feast, let the fun begin!"

A wisp of wind with a playful sweep,
Makes shadows dance and secrets seep.
The pumpkin joins, with a hearty cheer,
As spectral guests bring laughter near.

So tread with care, in fields so bright,
For ghostly giggles fill the night.
In every rustle, every sway,
Lies a jolly tale to brighten your way!

Veils of the Abandoned

In shadows where the tall weeds sway,
Old garden gnomes lost their way.
They frown and mumble, grumble too,
And tell bad jokes no one can view.

A trowel's lost, a spade's been stolen,
In this plot, the whimsy's swollen.
Flowers giggle, roots make a fuss,
Who knew plants could be so cussed?

Bugs in bow ties organize parades,
While spiders weave their escapades.
It's all quite mad, this leafy show,
With ghosts of daisies putting on a glow.

So if you wander near this patch,
Beware of wisps that wink and hatch.
For laughter echoes in the gloom,
In veils that hide a floral room.

Lament of the Lost Bloom

Once there bloomed a rose so grand,
Now it's a wilted hand.
With petals drooping, colors dim,
It tells its jokes in a sly whim.

"Oh woe!" it cries with a flourish flair,
"Life's a jest, or so I swear!"
Bees chuckle as they sip their tea,
At a posy's tragic comedy.

Each night the moon throws silver light,
On stems that dance in sheer delight.
A thyme that's lost will sing a tune,
To woo the ghosts who howl at noon.

With laughter echoed in the air,
They joke and tease without a care.
So raise a glass to blossoms gone,
And revel in their ghostly yawn.

Secrets Among the Thorns

Amidst the prickles and the grime,
The weeds hold secrets out of time.
With a wink, the bramble whispers true,
Of all the plants it once just knew.

The daisies plot a prank or two,
While violets giggle in the dew.
"Do they not see?" they tease and gloat,
The thorns, they wear their secret coat.

A wily vine dangles in jest,
Swinging high in carefree zest.
The sunflowers bow, a comical mood,
As shadows dance in leafy brood.

With shushed secrets held so tight,
The greenery holds a funny sight.
So venture close, but mind the sting,
For thorns can laugh, and have a swing.

Phantoms in the Underbrush

In the thicket where the wild things sing,
Frogs in tuxedos, a leafy fling.
They tap dance on logs and croak with glee,
As the fireflies shimmer, wild and free.

A ghostly cat with a purring grin,
Stalks the garden's secret din.
It chases shadows, slips with flair,
Leaving laughter floating in the air.

The owls chuckle from their trees,
As night brings stories on the breeze.
With giggly whispers, they lay their claim,
To the humor of this eerie game.

So stroll on through this wondrous scene,
Where phantoms play, if you know what I mean.
In the underbrush, the spirit glows,
In winks and nods from the world of woes.

When the Wind Carries Secrets

When whispers laugh among the trees,
You'd think the breeze has got the keys.
It tickles leaves with cheeky grace,
And plays tag with the clouds' soft lace.

A squirrel eavesdrops, eyes a-glint,
While flowers giggle, no hint of tint.
The daisies dance with secret flair,
As if they know someone's in the air.

The gusts are giddy, spirits wild,
Each gust just seems like nature's child.
Can wind transmit a silly rhyme?
Or do the trees just have good time?

Oh, if that breeze could tell a joke,
It'd have the crows around it choke.
With humor in the air so light,
The garden buzzes, day to night.

The Forgotten Corsage

A corsage lost upon the ground,
Forgetting scents my nose once found.
A bee just stung, it wasn't wise,
Now blooms wear frowns, with droopy eyes.

The chilly wind, it shakes the buds,
As if to say, 'Take care, you duds!'
Roses giggle, wilted in jest,
'You should wear me! I'm the best!'

Ferns twist and nod, with leafy flair,
'This fashion week, let's get some air!'
Yet all the blooms with vibrant tones,
Are tired now, they've lost their zones.

But somewhere near, an unseen friend,
Will toss a petal, spark to mend.
With laughter echoing through the spray,
The corsage dreams of brighter day.

Lullabies for the Unseen

In twilight's glow, the shadows play,
As creatures hum a soft ballet.
With twinkling stars, they sing a tune,
To serenade the sleepy moon.

The spiders weave their webs with care,
While crickets chirp a silent prayer.
The buzzing bees hum soft and sweet,
Lulling dreams on tiny feet.

If spirits danced on petals bright,
They'd giggle softly in the night.
A melody of whims and glee,
A symphony none else can see.

So close your eyes and drift away,
Let the unseen sing and play.
With every sigh the leaves will sway,
Embracing night 'til break of day.

Where Shadows Paint the Ground

In places where the shadows toss,
You'll see the laughter, feel the gloss.
A flicker here and wisp of there,
Makes sunlight dance without a care.

The garden tapers, tricks the eye,
With silly shapes that wave goodbye.
A squirrel leaps, a shadow's muse,
Where sunbeams boast and shadows bruise.

When puddles grin and raindrops sing,
You'll catch the joy that nature brings.
With ghostly friends that tease and chase,
They trick the mind, create a space.

So stroll beneath the leafy dome,
Where shadows feel they're free to roam.
In every corner, joy is found,
In whispering winds that twist around.

Twilight Blooms of Longing

In the twilight, flowers wink,
Petals giggle, making ink.
Breezes dance with silent whispers,
Tickled toes of unseen sisters.

Beneath the moon, mischievous vines,
Playfully twist on ancient pines.
Crickets chirp a silly tune,
As shadows prance beneath the moon.

A garden maze of prankster glee,
Where ghosts hide behind each tree.
They toss about their spectral laughs,
Chasing dreams like playful staffs.

Yet shadows flicker with a grin,
Haunted by where the fun begins.
With every bloom, the jesters bide,
In twilight's cloak, their glee resides.

The Lost Arbor's Caress

In an arbor where laughter plays,
Lost among the fragrant ways.
Branches tickle those who dare,
To venture forth without a care.

Rustling leaves in fitful chat,
Chasing squirrels, imagine that!
Ghostly giggles float on air,
Unseen phantoms wander there.

Beaming daisies grinning bright,
Nudging passers in the night.
Tales of whimsy echo near,
While specters stifle all their cheer.

Amidst the trunks, a secret jest,
A place where laughter knows no rest.
In shadows deep, the fun will steer,
Magic lives where none appear.

Treading Lightly Among Shadows

Treading lightly where shadows lie,
Ghostly whispers float on by.
Creeping plants with jokes to share,
Nudge my feet without a care.

Dandelions mock stern old trees,
Dancing in the softest breeze.
With every step, a chuckle's born,
As phantoms greet the breaking dawn.

Ticklish branches, lurking near,
Chuckle softly, 'Come, don't fear!'
They pull the pranks that make us laugh,
Turning gloom to a silly craft.

A twirl of night, a dance of light,
In silly games that feel just right.
While shadows play in playful jest,
I find the fun I love the best.

Enigma of the Hidden Gate

Behind the gate where secrets blend,
Lies a riddle with a twist to lend.
Ghostly figures stifle a giggle,
Acting out their little wiggle.

The blossoms laugh with silly grace,
In this odd and wondrous place.
With every push and playful tease,
The gate reveals its mysteries.

Snapdragons snap at wandering feet,
In this realm where phantoms greet.
The air is thick with laughter's trace,
Echoing joy from every space.

Yet if you peek to steal a glance,
You just might join their merry dance.
So tread with joy, embrace the fate,
In the realm behind the hidden gate.

The Spectral Fern's Embrace

In shadows where the ferns do sway,
The giggles of the lost come play.
They tickle the leaves, a breezy jest,
In this leafy haunt, they rest.

With phantom pranks and dances light,
They twirl around in the moon's soft bite.
A cheeky wink from beyond the day,
In ghostly whispers, they find their way.

Here lies a tale where laughter floats,
As sly spirits share their witty notes.
Each rustle a laugh, each leaf a sigh,
In spectral ferns, we learn to fly.

So visit this nook, where spirits tease,
With laughter echoing in the breeze.
For in the night, the past does gleam,
A comical pause in a timeless dream.

Lingering Whispers of the Past

In corners where the echoes play,
The whispers tickle, come what may.
A jest, a giggle, from times long gone,
In this surreal scene, we laugh along.

Old tales shared in hushed delight,
As shadows waltz in the pale moonlight.
The voices weave a funny charm,
With tricks and tales that disarm.

A pie thrown here, a shoe misplaced,
The spirits joke, no pride to waste.
They linger near, those mischief-makers,
In a soft breeze, eternal pranksters.

So heed the laughter in the air,
For ghosts love giggles; they're quite a pair.
Their witty ways we can't outlast,
In this curious dance, we're unsurpassed.

The Tenuous Veil of Memory

Behind the veil where thoughts reside,
The quirks of ghosts take us for a ride.
They tease our minds with riddles spry,
A chuckle forming with every sigh.

In wobbly paths of yesteryear,
Fleeting laughter echoes here.
Ghostly pranks like frozen tricks,
They dance to tunes of time's own flicks.

Backwards glances, an odd duet,
With headless jokes that we won't forget.
These slippery shadows share their wit,
In the delicate mist, they play a bit.

So don your garb of merriment bright,
And join the banquet of ghostly night.
Their mirthful riddles bridge the divide,
In this quirky realm, we confide.

Dusk's Haunting Caress

As dusk drapes its soft, quirky shroud,
The whispers rise, a giggling crowd.
With every rustle of leaves so light,
They craft a fancy for this twilight.

In soft chuckles, shadows play,
Turning the night into a cabaret.
Haunted laughs lift with each breeze,
In this funny world, they aim to please.

A game of tag with memory's hand,
With ghostly friends, we make our stand.
The night swells with tales absurd,
In the humor of gloom, we find our word.

So let the dawn come when it will,
For dusk's embrace—oh, what a thrill!
In laughter, we twine, and thus we stay,
In the late-night ballet, we find our play.

The Sylvan Cemetery

Among the trees, the shadows creep,
A place where laughter's lost its leap.
The squirrels tell tales, quite absurd,
Of beats from the past, to which we've erred.

The statues grin, with moss for hair,
They gossip loud, without a care.
One told a joke, it fell quite flat,
The crows just stared and called him 'fat'.

Here lies a poet, who tripped on words,
He never learned to chat with birds.
His rhyme was neat, but punchlines fled,
Now leaves conspire to make him dread.

With whimsy swirling upon the breeze,
The whispers chuckle among the trees.
In this odd realm where spirits jest,
Heavy were souls, but laughter's best.

Withering Echoes of Joy

In shadows casting silly pranks,
A ghost is dancing, full of flanks.
His moves are quite the sight today,
He tripped on roots, then slipped away.

The flowers giggle, bright and bold,
They tease the phantoms, young and old.
With petals waving, they declare,
'Join the fun! We don't have a care!'

The wind will carry a joke or two,
With every rustle, laughter grew.
As ivy vines twist round the fence,
They're bound to find the past makes no sense.

But here in this grove of fading light,
The echoes of cheer bring pure delight.
So let them laugh, in shades of gray,
For joy can linger, come what may.

Specters in the Wildflowers

In blooms where memories softly sway,
Past silhouettes come out to play.
Their antics, wild, bloom bright as sun,
As petals swirl, they have such fun.

One claimed to twirl, with such finesse,
But stumbled hard, creating mess.
The daisies laughed, the roses sighed,
'Oh dear ghost, let's hide your pride!'

A waltz among the lavender blooms,
With scent and giggles chasing gloom.
The butterflies flutter, what a sight,
While specters swing into the night.

They whisper jokes to pine and fern,
Each laugh a lesson that they learn.
In this wild patch, so lush and free,
Even lost souls find jubilee.

The Silent Thicket

In a thicket dense with silent laughs,
Ghostly figures plot their gaffes.
With tangled roots and vines that cling,
They whisper snickers, and faintly sing.

One phantasm tried to climb a tree,
And ended up falling, quite in spree.
The thrushes chirped, with quizzical eyes,
'Is it fall or flight?' their laughter flies.

Amidst the shadows, shadows play,
Each faded wink leads hearts astray.
They juggle clouds and moonlit beams,
In nighttime's hush, aroma streams.

So if you wander, heed the jest,
Among the quiet, spirits rest.
For in each pause, and every sigh,
The funny echoes never die.

Gossamer Threads of Memory

In a maze of whispers, I roam free,
Chasing shadows that giggle, you see.
A dancing specter, in mismatched shoes,
Leaves trails of laughter, the ghostly muse.

With each fluttering sigh, the past unfolds,
As poltergeists play with marigold.
Their cheeky pranks make time feel light,
While I'm bewitched by their spooky delight.

They swap my hat, wear it askew,
As I trip over roots where laughter grew.
Yet I can't help but chuckle low,
At these gossamer friends, all aglow.

In this spectral game we weave and play,
Each thread of memory leads astray.
Rooms of hilarity float on air,
Thanks to these quirky, yet charming, fare.

Faded Fragrance of Echoed Times

The scent of yesteryear tickles my nose,
With fragrant wishes planted like rows.
Old ghosts serve tea with a twist of lime,
And toast to memories lost in rhyme.

They giggle and dance in poltergeist cheer,
As echoes bounce around my ear.
'You forgot your purse!' one spirit yells,
While another concocts odd tales and spells.

A bumblebee buzzes with gossip to share,
As petals giggle, giving flowers a flair.
Each whiff of nostalgia brings up a grin,
In the realm of faint laughter, where fun begins.

They toss petals like confetti, oh so spry,
While time skips like a child, flapping by.
With whispers in the breeze, their laughter sways,
In this fragrant piece of yesterday's plays.

Enchanted Haze of the Abandoned

In the air, an animated fog appears,
Wrapped in chuckles, muffled cheers.
A rusty swing creaks with spectral fun,
As a ghostly kid pranks, just for the run.

Old oak trees wear hats of mossy green,
Barking out laughs that can't be seen.
They sway and bend, crafting shadows keen,
While weaving mischief, they reign supreme.

A crooked path leads past a charming sprite,
Who juggles moonbeams in the dying light.
Their giggles echo through this spooky maze,
Weaving tomfoolery in magical ways.

The wind carries tales of playful delight,
Where abandoned souls come out at night.
With every turn, I tumble and spin,
In this enchanted haze, the laughter begins.

Celestial Garden of Lost Souls

Under a celestial dome, the stars peek,
Cheeky phantoms giggle, a little unique.
They chase the comets, with joy in their stride,
In this heavenly nook, where spirits collide.

Flowers bloom brightly with radiant glee,
As ghostly gardeners dance around me.
They plant sprightly jokes in soil so kind,
As echoes of laughter through starlight unwind.

A mischievous breeze whispers secrets anew,
While twinkling lights flash in a comical hue.
Each twirl of the cosmos brings forth a prank,
In this fun-filled realm, all spirits are thunk.

So raise a toast to the phantoms with flair,
In this garden of wonders, where none have a care.
With starlit chuckles and memories old,
These lively lost souls, forever bold.

Faded Orchards of Time

Forgotten fruits hang low and ripe,
Silly shadows dance, a ghostly type.
Laughter echoes through twisted branches,
While lost souls trip in silly prances.

Swaying vines tell jokes from the past,
As time slips by, whimsical and fast.
Gnarled roots tickle, the spirits giggle,
In every creak, a ghostly wiggle.

Witty whispers flutter on the breeze,
Mirthful jesters among the trees.
Chasing squirrels with tales half-spoken,
In this orchard, laughter's never broken.

Juicy apples with a punchline,
Each one ripe for a ball of twine.
So grab a seat 'neath the old oak tree,
And join the jests of history.

Nightfall in the Enchanted Grove

As daylight dips, the frolic begins,
Whimsical spirits dance on a whim.
A moonlit stage where shadows reside,
Joined by laughter, with nowhere to hide.

Giggling fairies zip past like light,
Crickets chirp, making jesters take flight.
Each rustle's a joke tossed in the air,
What's that? Just a squirrel with flair!

Beneath the blooms where the starlight falls,
Banshees trade riddles and ancient calls.
With every gust, the ghosts take their leap,
Chasing their dreams, while the willows weep.

So grab a gourd and join the fun,
In this grove, the night's never done.
With the moon as our cozy lamp,
We're all just spirits, never a tramp!

Haunting Fragrance of Remembrance

A whiff of jasmine, a giggle in the air,
Flitting figures with mischief laid bare.
Sweet aromas weave tales of yore,
As comical phantoms burst through the door.

Whispers of sage tickle the nose,
While cheerful banshees share their woes.
With each sniff, the laughter grows loud,
A bouquet of joy, a ghostly crowd.

The marigolds chuckle as petals cascade,
Telling secrets of wearing charades.
Ghouls in their glory, pranking with zest,
In this fragrant haven, they throw a fest.

So, take a step in and breathe it all in,
Mirthful memories wrapped in a grin.
In this ethereal garden of cheer,
The scent of laughter will always be near.

Moonlit Paths of the Unseen

Under the glow where moonbeams twirl,
The unseen waltz with a fanciful whirl.
These paths are lined with giggling shades,
As mischief blooms, the darkness invades.

Footsteps echo in playful delight,
As shadows chase, crafting a fright.
But don't be scared, it's all in good fun,
Cheerful roundups when the day is done.

With lanterns swaying, they tell their tales,
Of funny moments, of wind and gales.
The night's a jest, a skit on repeat,
With each twist and turn, a playful beat.

So wander the paths, feel the moon's tease,
Join in the laughter, let down your knees.
For in this realm where shadows gleam,
Life's but a prank, an ethereal dream.

Resounding Footsteps on Ancient Paths

In the mist, they dance and play,
Old spirits skipping all the way.
With shadows long and laughter sweet,
They take the paths, on ghostly feet.

They trip on roots, then tumble down,
With hollow jokes, they haunt the town.
Adventurers lost with sighs and woes,
Just follow footsteps where no one goes.

Through whispers thick, they joke and jest,
In unseen games, they love the rest.
A parade of shades in frivolous cheer,
Inviting all to join, my dear!

They chase the light and hide in trees,
Making faces, just to tease.
With banter bold, they flirt and prance,
These spectral fools love to dance.

The Faded Path to Nowhere

Down the trail, no map in hand,
Those unseen pals can't understand.
With every step, a chuckle there,
They find fresh spots to stack despair.

Their jokes are lost, in echoes spun,
'What's worse than ghosts? A missing pun!'
But in this place of faded laughs,
The spirits find their silly paths.

Wandering near, they share a gaffe,
At thirty-six, they roll and laugh.
Those ghostly friends in stylish sprees,
Are always late for spectral tea!

So join the crew, if you are bold,
With tales of mischief to be told.
What joy to haunt this path you see,
Where feet aren't quite where they should be!

Looming Silhouettes in the Twilight

At dusk, they sway in wobbly lines,
Playing hide and seek with vines.
Heartbeats echo 'neath the stars,
Even shadows tease like friendly czars.

"Boo!" they shout, as you stroll near,
Yet all they want is ghostly cheer.
With goofy grins and midnight pranks,
They leap from shadows, giving thanks.

A shadow's wink makes spirits grin,
"Who's the ghost that let us in?"
With every leap and playful sight,
They dance until the morning light.

In twilight's glow, they whisper soft,
"Let's make a fuss and lift them aloft!"
With swirling laughs and just a touch,
Of crooked tricks, they love so much.

The Soft Murmur of Withered Leaves

Where leaves sit crisp and nice and dry,
The whispers blend, a ghostly sigh.
They swipe the air with playful glee,
Around the trees, they giggle free.

"Oh look! A rustle!" one will shout,
"Must be the wind; let's spin about!"
In swirling circles, they frolic loud,
Through empty fields, they've drawn a crowd.

Amidst the scrunch of crunchy gold,
They tell tall tales of spirits bold.
With goofy grins and wide-eyed charms,
They gather 'round with open arms.

So tread with care and watch your step,
These playful souls, in laughter, leapt.
For in their game, they hold the key,
To haunting fun—and just for free!

Specters Among the Petals

Butterflies whisper and waltz in the breeze,
A pumpkin with legs tries to peer through the trees.
Vines giggle and tangle, a cheeky old sprout,
While shadows do a jig, trying hard not to pout.

The roses wear spectacles, wise and polite,
As daisies call dibs on the best ghostly light.
A gopher in top hat cracks jokes with a worm,
Who dances on tiptoes with elegant charm.

Bumblebees buzzing with giggles and glee,
They serve dripping nectar like sweet smoky tea.
Their laughter's contagious, the daisies all sway,
As the sun sets in ruffles, and night steals the day.

So join in the laughter, just follow the tune,
As the flowers throw parties beneath the full moon.
With winks from the willows, the night comes alive,
Where even the phantoms find ways to survive.

Haunting Lilies of the Night

A lily in white wears a veil filled with fright,
Spinning sweet tales on a soft summer night.
With giggles and gasps, they dance on the grass,
While specters play peek-a-boo, hoping to pass.

Pond frogs are croaking their jokes in a row,
The fireflies flicker, putting on quite a show.
Old trees pretend to shiver, what a jest!
As crickets out-sing all the creatures' best quests.

The moon grins with mischief, a wink in its eye,
As shadows concoct games, just hoping to fly.
A riddle from roses, a game of charades,
While the phantoms put on their best masquerades.

Daffodils whisper with secrets galore,
They know all the pranks that the specters adore.
So join in the fun, let your spirit take flight,
In this funny old world of the lilies at night.

The Silent Orchard

Apples play hide-and-seek, lost in the leaves,
While ghosts munch on cider, they giggle and tease.
Old trees tell tall tales of time gone by,
As shadows slide softly, like clouds in the sky.

Cherries wear crowns of twinkling white lights,
Laughing as squirrels exchange silly insights.
Nuts roll with laughter, in barrels of fun,
While the breeze hums a tune that can't be outrun.

The pickers are playful, each basket a ball,
They juggle the harvest, then trip, and then fall.
Pumpkins dressed oddly roll down toward their fate,
With pumpkins in giggles, it's never too late.

So stroll through the orchard, let giggles resound,
As the phantoms share secrets of mischief they've found.
With each turn and twist, feel the warmth of delight,
As shadows abound, making laughter take flight.

Phantoms in the Ferns

The ferns wear their pajamas, looking so chic,
While ghosts play the sax, what a jazzy mystique.
Toadstools are dancing, they've got quite the beat,
As whispers tempt twirling with mischievous feet.

A hedgehog in sneakers runs fast with a grin,
Collecting odd trinkets he finds on the spin.
Old beetles in bow ties applaud the grand show,
As ladybugs sing, their performances flow.

Fireflies join in, lighting up the dark space,
Adding highlights of color, a whimsical grace.
As laughter erupts from the soft velvet air,
The ferns sway in rhythm, with ghosts everywhere.

So prance with the phantoms, embrace the surprise,
In a world of sweet secrets and glittering skies.
Let's dance with the shadows, in the fern's embrace,
Where joy intermingles, laughter sets the place.

The Absence of Flowering Light

In shadows where the daisies hide,
The silence sings, the crickets bide.
An absence here, a presence there,
The butterflies forget to care.

The sun forgot to kiss this patch,
While toadstools dance, and squirrels hatch.
The daisies wear their hats with flair,
Yet blooms are lost, a perfect scare.

The Flickering Lantern Among the Thorns

A lantern lit by wayward breeze,
Wobbles 'round like bats in trees.
With thorns that whisper lots of lies,
And roses rolling laughing cries.

The fireflies in tuxedos gleam,
As thorns keep plotting in their scheme.
What's blooming here? It's hard to say,
When laughter flies, and dreams delay.

Mourning in the Monochrome

In shades of gray where colors weep,
The garden sighs, it won't keep.
A parched petal, a heavy frown,
The weeds laugh loud, while blooms fall down.

The crows debate on life and worth,
As dandelions spring from earth.
What's missing here? A punchline's twist,
As monochrome drifts and laughs persist.

Ferns of Unfurling Secrets

Ferns unveil their secrets slow,
With whispers soft and giggles low.
Each curl exposes winks of glee,
In jest, they tease, oh can't you see?

A mantle green, a curtain shy,
With shadows flitting, spirits fly.
In jokes unheard in nature's tune,
The ferns will dance beneath the moon.

Remembering the Phantom Blooms

In twilight's haze, they twirl and spin,
With silly laughs, they grin and win.
Petals of laughter float in the air,
As playful whispers dance without care.

Each ghostly flower, a prankster's delight,
Lighting up the moon with mischief at night.
They tickle the breeze, a ticklish affair,
Smiles blooming brighter, everywhere.

Glowing mushrooms join in the fun,
Comedic shadows with no one to shun.
The wind tells jokes, a ghostly quip,
While the phantom blooms take a sassy sip.

As dawn's light fades this jolly jest,
Phantom blooms leave, a witty fest.
With giggles and tickles, off they go,
To haunt other gardens, putting on a show.

Dreams in the Tangled Thorns

In thorny thickets, dreams play hide-and-seek,
With laughter echoing, they're far from meek.
A jester's cap hangs from the prickly vines,
As shadows giggle, in whimsical lines.

Tangled memories, like yarn in a knot,
Thread by thread, the stories are caught.
Each thorny laugh a needle's delight,
Sewing the fabric of the starry night.

A dandelion sneeze sends specters awry,
They tumble and roll, beneath the sky.
In the midst of the thorns, jokes bloom so bright,
The garden of terrors just turns into light.

When morning arrives, dreams take their bow,
The tangled thorns enjoy the now.
With whispers of mirth on the morning air,
The thorns twirl around in a comical dare.

The Shadowed Bench

On a creaky bench where giggles live,
Shadows sneak in, just like they give.
They play musical chairs with unseen friends,
Bouncing and nodding as laughter bends.

The ghosts of chatter, they murmur and tease,
Telling tall tales with effortless ease.
People sit down, but not for long,
A ghostly nudge reveals where they belong.

With playful jests and a wink in their eye,
Phantoms amuse as they float on by.
Each creak of the wood, a story retold,
With mischief and glee, their antics unfold.

At dusk they disperse, the shadows take flight,
Leaving echoes of joy in the fading light.
The bench sighs softly, a job well done,
As laughter lingers, the day's just begun.

Veils of Faded Flora

In veils of color that shimmer and sway,
Faded flora giggles, come join in the play.
Blooming with puns, they sway in a dance,
Inviting the lost for a whimsical chance.

The petals would gossip, with each rustling breeze,
Creating a ruckus, a lively tease.
Their colors may fade, but the jokes are bright,
Warding off gloom with sheer delight.

Beside the crooked path, a flower can joke,
Sending the travelers into a choke.
They snicker and laugh as they flourish anew,
With echoes of joy that never feel blue.

As starlight drapes over leaves turned to gold,
The faded blooms whisper stories untold.
With giggle and grin, they fade into night,
Leaving behind bits of glittering light.

www.ingramcontent.com/pod-product-compliance
Lightning Source LLC
Chambersburg PA
CBHW071841160426
43209CB00003B/370